BRENT LIBRARIES

Please return/renew this item
by the last date shown.
Books may also be renewed by
phone or online.
Tel: 0115 929 3388
On-line www.brent.gov.uk/libraryservice

Here to Help

PARAMEDIC

Rachel Blount

Photography by Bobby Humphrey

W

FRANKLIN WATTS
LONDON•SYDNEY

Franklin Watts
First published in Great Britain in 2016 by The Watts Publishing Group

Credits
Series Editors: Rachel Blount and Paul Humphrey
Series Designer: D. R. ink
Photographer: Bobby Humphrey
Produced for Franklin Watts by Discovery Books Ltd.

Dewey number: 610.69
HB ISBN: 978 1 4451 4014 8
Library eBook ISBN: 978 1 4451 4015 5

Printed in China

Franklin Watts
An imprint of
Hachette Children's Group
Part of The Watts Publishing Group
Carmelite House
50 Victoria Embankment
London EC4Y 0DZ

An Hachette UK Company
www.hachette.co.uk

www.franklinwatts.co.uk

The publisher and packager would like to thank Nick Henry & West Midlands Ambulance Service, Jonathan Cobb & Zara Parkes, Headteacher David Porter and the staff and pupils of Belle Vue Primary School.

Contents

Words in **bold** are in the glossary on page 24.

I am a paramedic

My name is Jon and I am a paramedic. It is my job to help sick and injured people. I **respond** to **emergency** calls in an ambulance.

Hello!

How do you call for a paramedic?

This is where I work. It is called the **hub** for the West Midlands Ambulance Service.

Welcome to
Dudley Hub

I start work at 6:00 am and I book on with **control**. I get my ambulance keys and find out which ambulance I will drive today.

Next, I drive my ambulance to one of the **bases** in the area. Different ambulances go to different bases so they can respond to emergencies quickly.

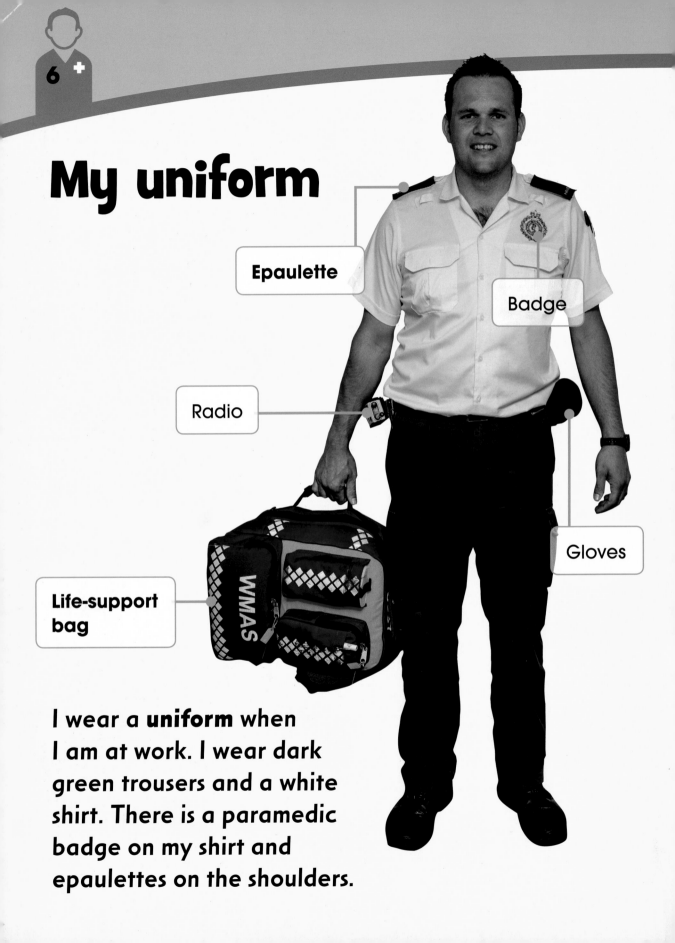

My uniform

Epaulette

Badge

Radio

Gloves

Life-support bag

I wear a **uniform** when I am at work. I wear dark green trousers and a white shirt. There is a paramedic badge on my shirt and epaulettes on the shoulders.

I also need some **equipment** to help me do my job.

Radio – I receive emergency calls from the **dispatch team** through my radio. I must carry it with me all the time.

Hard hat – If I am working in a dangerous place I wear a hard hat.

Life-support bag – My life-support bag is full of medical equipment and medicine to help me treat patients.

Gloves – I wear gloves to prevent **infection** when I am treating some injuries.

?

Why do paramedics wear a uniform?

Emergency vehicles

Paramedics use lots of different vehicles. There are vans, cars, motorbikes and even helicopters. Helicopters are used to get people to hospital more quickly than an ambulance can.

? Why are motorbikes and helicopters sometimes used by paramedics?

I drive a bright yellow and green ambulance. It has warning lights on the front and back that flash in an emergency. I sit in the cab in the front on the way to an emergency. I treat patients in the back on the way to hospital.

Warning lights

Heart monitor

Cab

Life-support bag

4216

West Midlands Am

Lift

Stretcher

4x4 ETS
Electronic Traction System

The side door slides open so we can get to the equipment quickly. At the back there is a lift to load the patient in on a stretcher.

Meet the team

I am usually **on duty** with another team member. Today I am working with Lian.

This is Pete. He is a **manager** and he helps to organise all of the ambulance staff on duty. He is also a trained paramedic.

Here are some of the other people who help out at the ambulance hub.

Mechanics like Lee help to keep the vehicles working properly.

I am checking the oil.

Ambulance fleet assistants like Martin help to clean and **restock** the ambulances when they have been used.

How does the team of people that Jon works with help him?

Emergency!

An emergency call comes through on the radio. Someone has been knocked off their bicycle. Lian puts the lights and **siren** on and we drive to the accident.

? When does the driver need to use the lights and siren on the ambulance?

I grab my life-support bag. A man is sitting on the ground next to his bike. He has hurt his arm. I need to check that he is OK. He might have a broken bone or **concussion**.

I talk to Keith to check that he is alert. I check and can see that Keith hasn't broken any bones, but he does have a nasty graze.

Keith feels better now. His wife is coming to take him home. I fill in a **patient report form**. I give a copy to Keith and say goodbye.

Another emergency

There is another emergency. A child called Zara has had an **allergic reaction** at school.

When I arrive at Zara's school, I ask her teacher what has happened. Zara was stung by a bee in the playground. Her mouth and throat are swollen.

I use the heart monitor to check her **pulse**. I also give her medicine through a needle in her hand.

Don't worry Zara.

We'll soon be at hospital.

Zara is struggling to breathe so I give her some **oxygen** through a mask. Zara needs to go to hospital. I help her on to the stretcher and push the button to raise the lift.

The teacher has called Zara's parents. They will meet us at the hospital.

?

Why do paramedics sometimes put patients on a stretcher?

To hospital

The ambulance siren and lights are turned on as we drive to hospital. It is sometimes quite bumpy, working on the move.

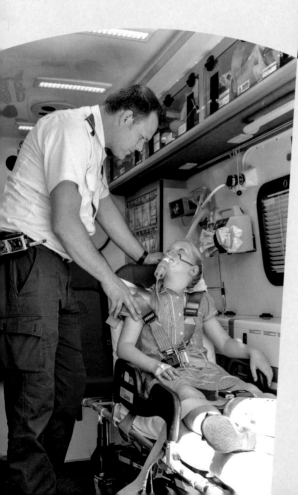

?

What should other road users do when they see an ambulance with its lights and sirens on?

I treat Zara in the back of the ambulance on the way to hospital. Her breathing has improved and the medicine I gave her has helped, too.

At hospital Zara is taken into the emergency department. I give the nurse in charge Zara's **notes**. The notes let the doctors and nurses know what treatment I have given Zara.

Your parents will soon be here, Zara.

Zara is feeling much better now and will soon be able to go home.

All sorts of emergencies

Paramedics get called to all sorts of emergencies. Here are just a few examples of the kind of emergencies that they attend.

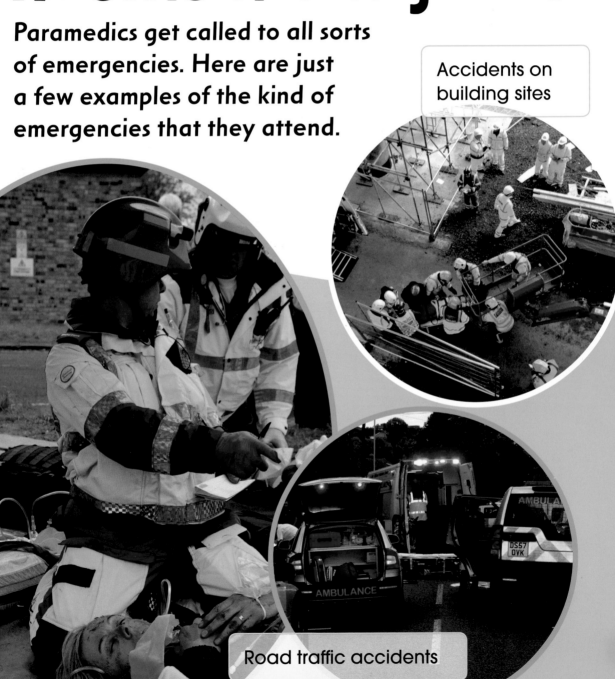

Accidents on building sites

Road traffic accidents

Farm accidents

Paramedics often work with other emergency services, such as the fire brigade, to help people whose lives are in danger.

In some emergencies it is important to call an ambulance but sometimes you may not need to ring 999.

You should call 999 if someone needs immediate medical attention and their life is in danger.

You should call 111 if someone urgently needs medical help or advice but their life is NOT in danger.

What happens when you dial 999?

End of the day

It has been a busy day, but there are still jobs to do. I drop the ambulance off with the fleet assistant at the hub. Martin will restock the ambulance and clean it.

Here are the keys, Martin.

Why do ambulances need to be cleaned after they have been used?

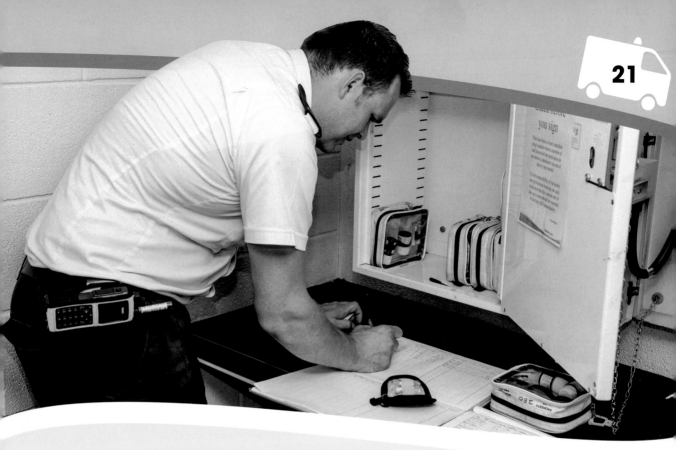

Next, I record what medicines have been used on a chart. Then I hand over the patient report forms to one of the managers, Martin.

It is 6:00 pm and time to go home. Paramedics work **shifts** so that we are available to attend emergency calls 24 hours a day.

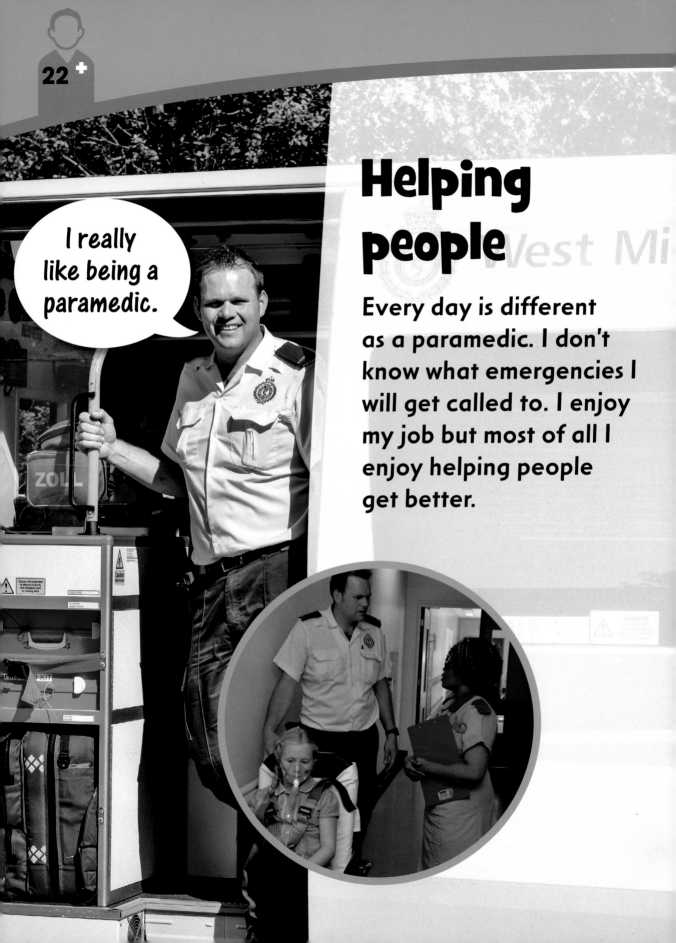

I really like being a paramedic.

Helping people

Every day is different as a paramedic. I don't know what emergencies I will get called to. I enjoy my job but most of all I enjoy helping people get better.

When you grow up...

If you would like to be a paramedic, here are some simple tips and advice.

What kind of person are you?

- You are kind and caring
- You are friendly and enjoy talking to people
- You are calm in an emergency
- You enjoy working as part of a team
- You are good at communicating with people
- Most of all, you enjoy helping people.

How do you become a paramedic?

- You can study for a degree in Paramedic Science at university.
- You can also study and train to be a paramedic with an ambulance service trust.
- You will need to achieve good GCSE grades in Maths, English and Science.
- You usually need two or three 'A' levels, including a science, to get onto a university course.

Answers

P4. Dial 999 in an emergency when someone needs urgent medical help. You will be asked whether you want the police, fire or ambulance service. Ask for the ambulance service.

P7. Paramedics wear a uniform so that people know who they are.

P8. Motorbikes and helicopters are faster than cars and vans, so they can get to emergencies quicker. They can also get to more difficult places that cars and vans can't reach.

P11. Jon's team help in many ways. They organise his work, make sure his ambulance is ready to use and help him attend emergencies and treat patients.

P12. The siren and lights are used when the ambulance is travelling to an emergency. They can also be used when taking a patient to hospital if they need to get there very quickly.

P15. Stretchers are used to transport some patients who are badly injured or are too ill to walk into the ambulance.

P16. Vehicles and cyclists should slow down and safely pull over to let an ambulance pass. Pedestrians should also be aware.

P19. You will be asked whether you need the police, fire or ambulance service and where you are.

P20. Cleaning the ambulances gets rid of any germs or blood that may have been left behind.

Were your answers the same as the ones in the book? Don't worry if they were different, sometimes there is more than one right answer. Talk about your answer with other people. Can you explain why you think your answer is right?

Glossary

allergic reaction when the body has a highly sensitive reaction to something

bases small ambulance stations spread around an area, such as a town or city

concussion temporary unconsciousness or confusion, sometimes caused by a knock to the head

control a room in the hub where the managers work

dispatch team people who receive emergency calls from the public and send paramedics to attend

emergency an unexpected and usually dangerous situation needing immediate action

epaulette a piece of material worn on the shoulder of a uniform

equipment objects that help paramedics to do their job

heart monitor an electronic piece of equipment used to monitor the function of the heart

hub a central place

infection an infectious disease

life-support bag a bag carried by a paramedic that contains essential medical equipment and medicine

manager someone who is responsible for an organisation or group of staff

mechanics people who repair and maintain vehicles

notes details about a patient's illness and treatment

on duty available to work

oxygen a gas that we need to breathe that is in the air around us

patient report form a form used by paramedics to record treatment

pulse the rhythm blood makes as it flows through arteries. You can feel a pulse in your neck or wrist

respond answer

restock to replace any medical equipment that has been used

shifts a set time when different groups of workers do the same job

siren a loud warning sound

uniform special clothing worn by people who belong to the same organisation

Index